GOOD VIBES ONLY

(...UNLESS YOU'RE A D*CK)

A Guided Workbook to Harness the Power of Positivity

I0809259

chartwell books

Quarto

© 2026 Quarto Publishing Group USA Inc.

This edition published in 2026 by Chartwell Books, an imprint of
The Quarto Group, 142 West 36th Street, 4th Floor, New York, NY 10018 USA
T (212) 779-4972
www.Quarto.com

Contains content originally published as *3-Minute Positivity Workbook* in 2023 by Chartwell Books.

All rights reserved. No part of this book may be reproduced in any form without written permission of the copyright owners. All images in this book have been reproduced with the knowledge and prior consent of the artists concerned, and no responsibility is accepted by the producer, publisher, or printer for any infringement of copyright or otherwise, arising from the contents of this publication. Every effort has been made to ensure that credits accurately comply with information supplied. We apologize for any inaccuracies that may have occurred and will resolve inaccurate or missing information in a subsequent reprinting of the book.

10 9 8 7 6 5 4 3 2 1

Chartwell titles are also available at discount for retail, wholesale, promotional, and bulk purchase. For details, contact the Special Sales Manager by email at specialsales@quarto.com or by mail at The Quarto Group, Attn: Special Sales Manager, 100 Cummings Center Suite 265D, Beverly, MA 01915, USA.

ISBN: 978-0-7858-4905-6

Publisher: Wendy Friedman
Publishing Director: Meredith Mennitt
Editor: Cathy Davis
Cover Designer: Brianna Tong
Interior Designer: Sue Boylan

Printed in Malaysia

This book provides general information. It should not be relied upon as recommending or promoting any specific diagnosis or method of treatment for a particular condition. It is not intended as a substitute for medical advice or for direct diagnosis and treatment of a medical or psychological condition by a qualified physician or therapist. Readers who have questions about a particular condition, possible treatments for that condition, or possible reactions from the condition or its treatment should consult a physician, therapist, or other qualified healthcare professional.

EEA Representation, WTS Tax d.o.o.,
Žanova ulica 3, 4000 Kranj, Slovenia.
www.wts-tax.si

GOOD VIBES ONLY

(...UNLESS YOU'RE A D*CK)

A Guided Workbook to Harness the Power of Positivity

chartwell books

Contents

Introduction

Positivity is not about being happy all the time (neither possible, nor desirable), not about avoiding negative events or feelings (things happen), not about pretending to be a happy, positive person (no fakes, please). Positivity is about becoming your best, authentic self, adopting a growth mindset, loving yourself and others, and acknowledging and managing your true feelings. It's also about learning to remain calm, focused, and solution oriented in challenging situations, maximally enjoying everything good in life, and improving your health. The more you practice positivity, the more it cycles back, doubling, tripling, and quadrupling positive thoughts and positive outcomes.

At birth, your brain already has special circuitry for experiencing joy, pleasure, and euphoria in place. Even if your environment fosters negativity and you've fallen deep into its trap, your brain has the capacity to change throughout your life. When you learn something new, your brain creates new neuronal networks to facilitate the use of that new knowledge.

Because thoughts and emotions trigger the desire for change—and provide the pathway to change—you can use both to wire your brain for increased positivity. You'll also need to act, but it all starts with conscious awareness of how your thoughts and feelings create your reality.

This workbook will offer you techniques designed to train your brain to focus on positivity, on ways to flip the negative to positive in all areas of your life. Each writing prompt or activity is designed to take only three minutes. First, information is provided to provoke thoughts and feelings, then you'll be asked to pick up your pen, set your timer, and write, or try an activity designed to bolster positivity. By the time you've completed this workbook, you'll be well on the way to retraining your brain to be far more optimistic, light-hearted, joyful, happy—and productive.

Because emotions are your primary source of information about how your life is working, or not, let's start there.

"Let's not forget that small emotions are the great captains of our lives, and that these we obey without knowing it."

—VINCENT VAN GOGH, ARTIST

1

Emotional Positivity

Emotions are often an unconscious reaction to an experience, based on how you experienced previous, similar incidents. The underlying, deeply felt emotion may drive how you feel, to the point that you seek therapy to discover the original incidents. Feelings are a conscious reaction to emotional or physical sensations, which means you have greater ability to choose how you feel.

Positive and negative emotions play important roles in how our brain processes information, and these roles are complementary rather than competitive. Positive emotions have been shown to impact the brain by:

- Stimulating feel-good hormones that both calm your brain and lift your spirits (your positivity!).
- Boosting cognitive performance. Negative emotions distract your brain, making it harder to think or concentrate.
- Lowering stress hormones and promoting a sense of well-being.
- Broadening your horizons and widening your brain's scope of focus.

Meanwhile, negative emotions can also have *positive* effects on your brain by:

- Helping you manage challenging situations by teaching you how to process conflict and make sense of incongruent or conflicting emotional information.
- Helping you cognitively sort confusing signals (someone is saying one thing, but you're feeling another).
- Helping you form stronger emotional boundaries by limiting empathy, when necessary.

One big way to gain control of your emotions is to understand their capacity as messengers, and to appreciate the positive benefits they bring.

COMMON POSITIVE EMOTIONS

happiness
serenity
amusement
love
joy
contentment
interest
awe
satisfaction

COMMON NEGATIVE EMOTIONS

disgust
annoyance
loneliness
sadness
rage
fear
jealousy
anger
melancholiness

All Emotions Serve a Purpose

Remember, emotions are instructive indicators of what requires your focus. They let you know when someone crosses an important boundary, when it might be dangerous to trust someone, when you are safe enough to relax, what it feels like to be loved. They let you know if you hate what you are doing, if you're being asked to do something that goes against your conscience, or if what you're doing restores your soul. Here are some examples of how emotions help:

Anger: helps you stand up for yourself.

Fear: alerts you to danger.

Anticipation: doubles your happiness by "dreaming ahead."

Surprise: jolts you into the present and delights you.

Joy: reminds you what makes you happy and how good it feels to be happy.

Sadness: helps you grieve loss.

Trust: helps you form intimate relationships and builds your confidence.

Disgust: alerts you to things that violate your sense of self and sets parameters.

Loneliness: drives you to connect with others.

Love: fulfills biological (reproduction) and sociological urges (connection, stable relationships, security, caring, community).

Now, see if you can identify at least three ways each of the following emotions might be helpful in your life:

Anger:
1.

2.

3.

Fear:
1.

2.

3.

Anticipation:
1.

2.

3.

Surprise:

1.

2.

3.

Joy:

1.

2.

3.

Sadness:

1.

2.

3.

Trust:

1.

2.

3.

Disgust:
1.

2.

3.

Loneliness:
1.

2.

3.

AN EMOTION BY ANY OTHER NAME

What we call emotions today have always been analyzed, beginning in Ancient Greece, under a variety of language-specific labels that include: passion, sentiment, affection, affect, disturbance, movement, perturbation, upheaval, or appetite.

Love:
1.

2.

3.

So, let's explore your emotions: Make a list of ten emotions you most often experience. Put stars by the positive ones.

1.

2.

3.

4.

5.

6.

7.

8.

9.

10.

Write about the top five negative emotions that tend to trip you up. Don't judge, just try to identify the triggers —when and why they happen.

1.

2.

3.

4.

5.

Based on your previous list of five negative emotions, write about what each of those emotions might be trying to tell you.

1.

2.

3.

4.

5.

COMMON ANGER TRIGGERS

If you listed anger as a negative emotion, see if the triggers listed below make you angry.

- Feeling like you are being disrespected, not seen, heard, or understood.
- Feeling like others are making unfair decisions that involve you.
- Feeling anxious, frightened, fearful, or abused.
- Being told to "calm down" so you will stop talking or reacting.
- Being constantly interrupted when trying to express your thoughts.
- Having someone overstep your boundaries and do or say something that negatively affects you without your permission.
- Wanting to do something and being told you cannot.

It's helpful to think about what triggers your anger and if it's the appropriate response. The essential questions to ask yourself would be: *"Is your anger helpful?"* and *"Are you listening to what it's telling you?"*

Are Your Negative Emotions Instructive?

Negative emotions help us survive and help us grow and develop as people—if they're instructive. They also offer a counterpoint to positive emotions: without ever feeling sad, would you love feeling joyful quite as much as you do? Ideally, you'll learn to fully savor your positive emotions—and all the positivity goodies they bring—and tamp down your negative emotions, avoid knee-jerk reactions, and better manage your emotions. The goal is to identify your negative emotions when they occur, step back, contemplate what caused them, address the situation to your advantage, and choose a healthier, more positive, or rewarding way to respond in the future.

If you are letting these emotions overly influence your current emotional reactions (inappropriately), it can be helpful to write about how that happens. Here are writing prompts to get you started:

> "Anger is an assertion of rights and worth...In anger, whether you like it or not, there is truth."
>
> —SORAYA CHEMALY, *RAGE BECOMES HER*

Write about the last time you felt sadness. What triggered that feeling?

How did you feel while sad?

Can you remember a time when you were a child and felt particularly sad?

Were your feelings/reaction appropriate to the situation? Is some of that sadness creeping into how you feel when you're sad now?

In the latest instance, was the level of your sadness appropriate?

Was your response appropriate?

Did you wallow? Do you find that wallowing is a productive response? If so, why?

Write about the last time you felt lonely. What triggered that feeling?

Were you alone a lot as a child?

Write about how that felt and what you did. Do you still respond to your lonely feelings the same way?

Write about a time you were alone but not lonely.

Identify the difference. Were you doing something you love? Were you simply tired?

List five ways you can enjoy solitude in the future.

1.

2.

3.

4.

5.

Write about the last time you felt disgusted.

Were the judgments you made fair? If yes, what did you learn about yourself?

Write about how you've used feelings of disgust with others to set boundaries.

How has it helped you change your own behavior?

Write about your last outburst of anger. What happened?

How did you respond?

VALUE YOUR EMOTIONS

Emotions affect attitudes, values, and beliefs we formulate about people, the world, things, ourselves, and things that happen to us or around us. Without emotions, your attitudes, values, and beliefs would be statements devoid of meaning.

Can you identify the underlying cause/trigger of your anger?

Were other feelings involved, such as frustration, disappointment, or fear?

Looking back now, how could you choose to act differently?

What steps can you take to productively express your anger?

What would be the risk in taking those steps?

What's Bugging You Most?

Use the space below to similarly explore emotions that regularly cause you distress or pain, particularly in situations where your reaction seems inappropriate or excessive:

Enraged:

Fearful:

Abandoned:

Anxious:

Tense:

Disappointed:

Discouraged:

Lethargic:

Disconnected:

Depressed:

Are You Seeing a Pattern?

Remember, the primary reason negative emotions exist is to focus your attention on areas of your life that are causing you pain. If you're feeling overwhelmed by negative emotions on an almost daily basis, it's time to use those feelings to identify the areas of your life that need attention.

Write about five specific problem areas causing your negative emotions.

1.

2.

3.

4.

5.

Identify the ones you want to, or can, change.

Write about how you specifically want each issue to change.

1.

2.

3.

4.

5.

Write down four ideas you have for implementing the changes required.

1.

2.

3.

4.

tip

NAME THAT EMOTION

The next time you are swept up in a strong emotion, pause and take a few slow, deep breaths. See if you can identify what your true emotion might be. Are you angry? Or are you disappointed and hurt? Naming your emotions help you address the real problem, and often prevent unfair accusations that can lead to escalating the situation.

Call Upon Your Thinking Brain

Once you have named your primary emotion, your prefrontal cortex helps you make cognitive interpretations, to identify the specific emotion you are feeling, and then identify the cause of the emotion. You can also learn to ponder whether the level of emotion you felt was appropriate, over-reactive, nonproductive, or dangerous. This cognitive appraisal helps you experience and feel a larger, more complex set of emotions. For each primary emotion listed, some of the secondary emotions you could feel might be:

Fear: anxious, nervous, skeptical, afraid, alarmed, terrorized.

Anger: tense, distressed, antagonized, alarmed, incensed, enraged, rageful, murderous.

Annoyance: Dissatisfied, irritated, discouraged, miserable, provoked, infuriated.

Sadness: Bored, lethargic, tired, dispirited, disconnected, deprived, abandoned.

Love: admiration, infatuation, attraction, fondness, friendship, devotion, worship.

Contentedness: full, pleased, gratified, relaxed, calm, satisfied.

Happiness: Delighted, glad, pleased, amused, excited, astonished.

"Until you
make the
unconscious
conscious,
it will direct
your life and
you will
call it fate."

– CARL JUNG,
PSYCHIATRIST
AND AUTHOR

So, let's explore some of your more negative emotions. Start with the primary emotions and work towards secondary emotions.

Make a list of negative emotional fluctuations you often struggle to overcome. Start with the primary emotion and see if you can more correctly identify whether the secondary emotion you experienced was more rage or incensed disappointment.

Write about past memories or underlying feelings that cause those emotions.

tip

NAME THEM TO TAME THEM

Naming emotions pauses reactivity, calms your reactive amygdala (feeling brain), and engages your frontal cortex (thinking brain). When you feel overwhelmed, first, breathe deeply, then pause to name the specific emotion. Naming it reduces the sting, helps you recognize subtlety, and helps you identify your emotional setpoint (the point at which you lose control).

Make a list of ways you can address the cause of your negative emotional response.

tip

STOP BLAMING

When arguing, it's always helpful to avoid personal attacks by owning and addressing your feelings. You do this by not saying: "You're always late" and instead saying "I am feeling devalued because it took so long for you to show up." Stick to your real issue, not your reactive emotion.

CREATE A PERSONAL MANTRA:

When negative feelings or thoughts just won't stop, your own mantra can both distract your mind and redirect it towards positivity. Take three minutes to create a mantra that will help you calm down in emotional situations. It could be a reassuring statement, such as "I am peace and light," or a philosophical statement, "Nothing good comes of anger." It can be anything you want, just make sure it stimulates positivity. When your emotions spiral out of control, chant (silently, if necessary) your mantra for three minutes.

"Strengthening neural systems is not fundamentally different [than strengthening certain muscle systems through physical exercise]. It's basically replacing certain habits of mind with other habits."

– RICHARD DAVIDSON, PHD,
THE EMOTIONAL LIFE OF YOUR BRAIN

2

Mental Positivity

One cognitive theory of emotion posits that your thoughts create your emotions. Another theory, called cognitive appraisal theory, suggests that someone must first think before experiencing an emotion. It's also possible that a physical reaction (a thundering heart at the sight of a lion) led to your fear. Or someone crept up behind you, yelled "boo," and your soaring heart rate caused your body to experience fear. In most cases, it's your thoughts about what's happening (and what happened in your past) that determine the emotion you feel.

WHY YOU REACT THE SAME WAY EVERY TIME:

Previous events (conscious or unconscious) wire emotional memories to certain stimuli. When something new stimulates the same neuronal territory, your emotional brain often sends you down the familiar "neuronal pathway," which causes you to respond to the new stimulus the same way you typically respond. You can use your thinking brain to intervene and create a new, more desirable response. If you repeatedly practice that more desirable response, it will soon form its own neural pathway.

Five Ways Emotions Move Us

Emotions have five components that happen (almost) simultaneously:

1. Your brain engages: You see, hear, smell, or otherwise sense danger, or a perceived threat.

2. Autonomic physiological changes: Your heart rate increases, you sweat, you feel dizzy, and these changes happen whether you want them to or not.

3. An action: You might gasp, scream, or weep, or you might suppress it.

4. A motor expression: You fight back verbally or physically, you run away, you put up your hands to protect yourself, and these actions are usually instinctive, though they can be how you reacted when you first felt fear, anger, frustration, love, or joy.

5. A subjective feeling: You feel frightened, angry, loved, upset, or sad—an emotional response based on life experiences. It also means that you can sometimes choose how you want to feel, or at least modulate the level of your response. This requires engaging your prefrontal (thinking) cortex. You may still feel angry, but you can lower the intensity and choose how fiercely you react.

While all or most of these reactions happen automatically, you have a choice as to how you feel and respond to your emotions.

Are You Obsessed with Controlling Your Emotions?

We often struggle to control situations, other people, how we behave in certain situations, and our own emotions. Alas, we often fail. According to the authors of *Stop Avoiding Stuff*, we have less control than we'd like to think. They suggest that the things you have little control over are:

- Thoughts that arise spontaneously.
- Emotions that arise spontaneously.
- Physical sensations, urges, and memories that arise spontaneously.
- The thoughts and feelings of others.
- What other people do and say.
- Your immediate circumstances.
- Your past.
- Your future.

What you can control are:

- How you respond to your thoughts (noticing/accepting/arguing with them).
- How your respond to your emotions (allowing them in/pushing them away).
- How you respond to sensations, urges, and memories (accepting them as normal/rejecting them).
- How you respond to your circumstances (problem solving, appreciating).
- How you act towards others (kind, dismissive, attentive, loving, cold).
- What you choose to make important in your life (family, work, play).

Let's explore your obsession with control:
What (or whom) do you secretly wish you could control?

Write about your obsessive needs to control. How does it feel in your body? Your mind?

What frustrates you most about not having control?

[3-MINUTE ACTIVITY]

SHORT-CIRCUIT NEGATIVITY

The next time you find yourself ruminating on everything bad that's happened in your life, consider the butterfly meditation, which you can do anywhere, anytime. Simply set a timer for 3 minutes and find a quiet spot. Calm your body, sit comfortably, place your hands on your lap (or touch your index fingertips to your thumb tips), breathe slowly in and out for a minute. Then allow your negative thoughts to surface, and without engaging in any way, envision each thought is a butterfly, and simply observe them fluttering away into the stratosphere.

When was the last time you lost control of your emotions? What happened? How did it feel?

List ten things (or people) you need to stop trying to control.

1.

2.

3.

4.

5.

6.

7.

8.

9.

10.

List ten things you can have some measure of control over.

1.

2.

3.

4.

5.

6.

7.

8.

9.

10.

Wire Your Brain for Positivity

There's nothing your brain likes more than those feel-good hormones it produces when you're feeling pleasure. It bathes itself in them and begs for more. To increase positivity, add a fun activity to what you don't like doing. If you hate cleaning on a Saturday morning, pick up a gourmet lunch and have a picnic after you clean. If you find exercising gruesome, call someone who always makes you laugh right after you've worked out. Linking pleasure to something unpleasant bathes your brain in the hormones that make it—and you—feel so good. Soon, both you and your brain won't mind those activities half as much.

List five things you hate doing and write about why you hate doing them. What makes those tasks so tedious?

1.

2.

3.

4.

5.

Did you always hate them? If not, what changed?

Write anything that you like about doing them. Look for something positive!

1.

2.

3.

4.

5.

List the rewards you get from doing them. A clean house, an organized life, a healthier body, etc.

1.

2.

3.

4.

5.

List five fun things you could do right after each of those activities and why that would be pleasurable.

1.

2.

3.

4.

5

tip

REWIRE YOUR BRAIN

Start wiring your brain for pleasure right now. Get a snack or treat and reward yourself for writing in this workbook.

Try Mindfulness to Enhance Awareness

Although it might sound intimidating, mindfulness is simply the practice of remaining mindfully aware of what's happening in your present moment—rather than allowing your mind to be distracted, wander, ruminate about your past, or fantasize about your future. Being mindful means being aware of your surroundings and what is occurring, while also staying finely attuned to what you are thinking and feeling in the present moment. Being mindful means being responsible moment by moment, for the inner workings of your mind. Mastering mindfulness will help you control your mind, rather than allowing your mind to control you.

"Mindfulness helps you go home to the present. And every time you go there and recognize a condition of happiness that you have, happiness comes."

– THICH NHAT HANH, BUDDHIST MONK AND AUTHOR

A MINDFULNESS BRAIN IS A HAPPY BRAIN

Studies of Tibetan Buddhists, dedicated mindfulness meditators, and the happiest people alive, found that their brains were highly focused on intention and revealed sharpened awareness and increased empathy—qualities essential to happiness—while meditating and long after meditating. You don't have to meditate as ardently as Tibetan Buddhists, but regular meditation will boost positivity.

Mindfulness meditation (which we'll discuss next) teaches you the following:

1. How to pay attention in a particular way.
2. How to pay attention and stay alert.
3. How to dismiss distractions and direct your thoughts.
4. How to monitor and redirect your emotions.
5. How to create a goal and exert mind control to make it happen.

Engaging in mindfulness meditation means creating an intention and motivation for your mind to alter the way it perceives, receives, and reacts to thoughts and emotions. It helps you train your mind and your brain to observe and embrace (or deflect) anything and everything that comes to your mind, sans judgment and with acceptance and openness.

Start with a Beginning Mindfulness Meditation

Mindfulness meditation is a meditation focused on exploring your thinking and feeling process. It's designed to bring all thoughts back inside, allowing you to better control your thoughts, feelings, and actions. If you've never mindfully meditated before, start here:

1. Find a quiet, peaceful place to sit comfortably. You don't have to sit with your legs crossed under you. Just sit comfortably and quietly, away from others, if possible.
2. Close your eyes, take a few slow, deep breaths. As you do so, focus on the rise and fall of your chest as each breath comes in and then goes out.
3. Continue your slow, steady breath. Move your attention to your stomach and notice how it rises and falls with each breath.
4. As thoughts occur (and they will!), notice them, but release them and refocus on your breath.
5. Do this for three to five minutes, and then slowly build up your time.

It's said two twenty-minute sessions a day will boost positivity and the ability to better control how your mind processes thoughts and how you manage your emotions. Allow yourself to start slowly and build to the twenty minutes, twice a day.

> "Set your course by the stars, not by the lights of every passing ship."
>
> – GENERAL OMAR N. BRADLEY

PRACTICE MINDFULNESS MEDITATION

Taking time to mindfully meditate boosts positivity because it:

- Boosts activity in your cerebral cortex, which helps reduce anxiety and regulate emotions.
- Reduces negative rumination and helps you stop negative thought spirals that can lead to depression and self-sabotage.
- Improves awareness and self-control, which helps you manage compulsive behaviors such as phobias, anxiety, overeating, drinking too much alcohol, and worrying.
- Helps you learn to be in the present moment and focus your thoughts.
- The more you practice mindfulness meditation, the more you wire your brain for positivity.

Try These Mindfulness Meditations

According to Tara Brach, in *Radical Compassion*, mindfulness involves two key questions: "What (feeling) is happening inside me?" and "Can I 'be with this' or can I 'let this be?'" Keep this in mind as you try the following beginner mindfulness meditations.

- Take three minutes and focus on your breathing. Don't make any effort to change or control it; just observe your breath. Try not to think about anything while you focus. When a thought surfaces (and it will), dismiss it, and go back to simply observing your breath.
- Take three minutes and scan your body. Modulate your breath so it's moving in and out at a slower pace. Bring your attention to the top of your head, then slowly scan down to your face, your neck, your shoulders, your arms, your chest, down your body until you reach your feet. Slowly repeat, going from your feet to the top of your head. This is simply an exercise about focusing your attention on what may be happening in your body. With more practice, you will sense what your body is feeling in the moment.

BONUS BENEFITS

In addition to bolstering positivity, mindfulness and meditation also help you balance your state of mind, increase creativity, increase your sense of peace, increase your awareness, elevate your consciousness, and build confidence and wisdom.

- Fetch a delicious snack and then spend three minutes focused solely on how it looks, how it tastes, and how it feels to slowly savor it. Slowly bite into it, chew slowly, feel its texture and taste, savor its goodness, then swallow and repeat. This brings your focus to the sensations important to appreciating nourishment and the pleasure it brings.
- Move mindfully by lifting your arms into the air. Spend three minutes slowly raising both arms, stretching them upwards as high as you can, holding them for a few breaths and then slowly lowering them. Repeat. As you move, notice how good it feels to simply move, how it makes your blood flow, how your muscles feel as they elongate and retract, how good it feels to lower them again. This builds appreciation for movement and bolsters body awareness.
- Take three minutes to do what's called a "loving meditation." This involves quieting yourself, surrendering all thoughts so you can focus solely on loving yourself. Wrap your arms around yourself and gently hug or touch your face. Offer yourself loving thoughts and ask yourself how you can love yourself better.

Write down five ways you can better love yourself. Be specific.

1. ______
2. ______
3. ______
4. ______
5. ______

Take three minutes to send a loving meditation to others. Again, sit comfortably, quiet yourself, and focus on your breathing until you can stop all interfering thoughts. Then send loving thoughts to friends, family, coworkers, acquaintances, and anyone who needs to feel loved.

Use Cognitive Behavior Therapy to Focus Your Thoughts

American psychiatrist Aaron T. Beck developed Cognitive Behavior Therapy (CBT) as a method for changing thoughts and behaviors to improve positivity. He believed having negative thoughts about yourself caused unnecessary psychological distress, and that changing the way you processed your thoughts could circumvent those results. His therapy focuses on breaking the cycle of negative thinking. Here are some CBT exercises.

1. Distract your thoughts.

a) Take three minutes to remember an event in your recent past that caused distress. Put yourself back in that moment, allowing yourself to delve into the feelings of that moment.

b) Now, distract your mind by taking three minutes to do something fun or gratifying. Polish your fingernails, wash your face, call your grandmother, kiss your children, hug your spouse or partner. Notice how quickly you can distract your mind from negative to positive thoughts. Practice this whenever you're caught up in negative thinking.

2. Try guided imagery.

a) Write a list of three events that made you extremely happy.

1. ______________________________

____

2. ______________________________

____

3. ______________________________

b) Take three minutes to remember one in vivid detail, taking your mind on a trip backwards, feeling, seeing, and tasting each moment. Allow all that warmth and happiness to bathe you in good feelings. Use this technique when negativity rears its ugly little head.

3. Neutralize negative thoughts.

a) Often, in stressful situations, we allow our minds to leap to the worst possible outcome. Take a few minutes to think about a situation you're currently worried about. Write down what your anxious mind thinks is the "worst" that may happen.

b) Now, pause to call on your rational mind and write what it thinks will realistically happen.

c) List areas in your life where you may be leaping to the worst conclusions.

1.
2.
3.
4.
5.

d) Write down your worst thoughts or imaginings.

1.
2.
3.

e) Replace your fearful thoughts with more realistic outcomes.

1.
2.
3.

4. Neutralize negative self-talk.

a) Take a few minutes to think about a recent time when you allowed your mind to bombard you with negative self-talk. Write what you "heard" your anxious self say about you.

b) Now take those thoughts and rewrite them in far more supportive, positive ways.

c) Make a list of at least five negative words you tend to use.

1.
2.
3.
4.
5.

d) Make a list that flips those words to positive words.

1. ______
2. ______
3. ______
4. ______
5. ______

5. Practice thought stopping.

a) Take a few minutes to think about something that brought you down in recent days. Go ahead and brood for a few minutes. Envision or write about what happened.

______

______

b) After three minutes brooding, hold up your hand and say aloud, "stop!" Use this as a clear directive to your mind that your conscious self wants it to stop focusing on negative thoughts. Use this whenever you feel caught in a negative thought spiral.

6. Practice reframing your thoughts.

a) Take a few minutes to think about a recent event that felt terrible at the time. Write about it.

______

______

b) Now, take a moment and see if you can reframe how you think about the event. Try identifying a positive outcome, or understanding more about what might have caused that event to be terrible. The more you find the positive aspect in painful events, the more often you'll reframe negativity to positivity.

7. Create positive affirmations.

a) Take a few minutes to think about an upcoming event that you're nervous about. Really dig into your fears and allow yourself to imagine the worst. Write it down.

____

b) Now take three minutes and write about the best way that same event could unfold. Write it down.

____

c) Meditate for three minutes. See the positive outcome unfolding, see it in detail, step-by-step. Feel how happy you'll be when the best, rather than the worst, happens.

d) Write down what you want to happen in the form of an affirmation, as if it's already happened exactly the way you want.

____

8. Break the opinionated habit.

a) Make a list of five negative opinions you tend to repeat in social situations, mostly without pausing to think.

1. ______________________________
2. ______________________________
3. ______________________________
4. ______________________________
5. ______________________________

b) Evaluate each opinion. Is it based on fact? Could you possibly be wrong?

c) Cross off the opinions that seem particularly negative. Either rewrite them or strive to eliminate them from your social repertoire.

9. Release negative stories.

a) List the top five negative stories you tend to tell over and over (to illustrate how cruel the world has been to you).

1.
2.
3.
4.
5.

b) Can you eliminate any of those stories?

c) Can you reframe them to be more positive? Write about whatever good may have come out of those situations. What did you learn?

1.
2.
3.
4.
5.

d) Take time to meditate on each story and see if you can accept what happened and forgive anyone who hurt you. Write a vow to forgive and forget.

e) Create a list of five positive stories you can share about yourself in social situations.

1.
2.
3.
4.
5.

"The key is to remember that how our minds feel as we go about our day—how relaxed, happy, and fulfilled we are—gets translated into the physiology of the body."

– LISSA RANKIN, *THE FEAR CURE*

3

Physical Positivity

Positive thinking has immediate and long-lasting effects on our health. Not only does it decrease the chance you'll succumb to negativity, anxiety, isolation, or depression, it helps relieve stressors in your life, like those you'll experience at work and at home. Many studies have shown that optimists enjoy better health than pessimists. Studies have even shown a correlation between positive thinking and longevity. Positivity provides many health benefits, some of which are:

- A longer life span.
- A lower chance of having a heart attack.
- Lower blood pressure.
- Lower stress hormones.
- Better physical health.
- Greater resistance to illnesses such as the common cold.
- Better pain tolerance.

The more positivity you train your brain to feel, the longer you'll live. Here's to a long, happy life!

So, let's talk about your health:

Do you have health concerns? What are they? List your top five concerns, or what you'd like to improve.

1.

2.

3.

4.

5.

Write about your fears around these concerns.

List five ways you can begin to address these concerns.

1.

2.

3.

4.

5.

Are you being evasive, avoiding something crucial? Admit to it here.

Why are you protecting yourself from the truth? Guilt? Stubbornness? Lack of knowledge?

How can you face up to your health challenge (the one you want to deny)?

FOUR WAYS EXERCISE BOOSTS MENTAL ACUITY

Exercise does amazing things for your body. Simple walking counts, speed walking alternated with slow walking really counts. Exercise:

- Stimulates blood flow, which keeps your brain receptive, flexible, and sharp.
- Activates your cerebellum, which helps you think faster and better.
- Increases self-confidence and self-esteem.
- Stimulates neural growth factors that improve function.

It doesn't matter what you do, just move your body on a regular basis. The more you move, for increasingly longer periods of time, the more you stimulate your brain.

It's Not About Weight, It's About Health

Focus on treating your body well because you love it, not because you want to change it. It's not about ignoring health risks (address those with your doctor, please), but about shifting your focus from punishing yourself to loving yourself enough to enhance self-care.

What's Your Emotional Connection?

If you eat or drink too much when you're emotionally upset (lonely, hurt, angry, sad, or frustrated), you've linked eating, or drinking, to negative emotions; and if it's left you unhappy with your body, your consolation prize is only making you feel worse. Ask yourself these questions:
If you eat too much, or drink too much, or regularly eat foods you know are very unhealthy, why?

"Keeping your body healthy is an expression of gratitude to the whole cosmos—the trees, the clouds, everything."

– THICH NHAT HANH,
BUDDHIST MONK AND AUTHOR

Have you always connected food or alcohol with certain emotions? When did this start? Write about your worst experiences.

How bad is it now? Be honest with yourself on this.

Can you identify which emotions commonly trigger the destructive behavior?

Can you recall an early memory connected to eating inappropriate food, or eating too much food?

Were you attempting to suppress an emotion when you drank too much? Can you identify the emotions and their triggers?

Take a moment to envision how each scene might have played out differently. What could you (or your caregiver) have done instead?

When was the last time you abused food or alcohol? What happened?

How did it make you feel? Write about the negative feelings attached.

Can you envision making different choices? How would that look?

NO HAPPY EXCUSES

Overeating or overdrinking when happy is also a problem. Connecting any strong emotions to eating or drinking adds an undesirable charge to what your body needs for sustenance or what can become harmful. It's fine, of course, to treat yourself occasionally, but the ability to regularly choose moderation means you are maintaining a proper perspective.

Step Away from Self-Sabotage

Doing anything that results in hurting the body you are attempting to nurture is self-sabotage. You could be overeating, overdrinking, not exercising, not getting enough sleep, not doing activities to recharge, or not making time for yourself.

If it makes you feel bad, it's hurting you. List five ways you currently self-sabotage.

1.

2.

3.

4.

5.

"Don't turn away. Keep your gaze on the bandaged place. That's where the light enters you."

– RUMI, POET

Love yourself instead. List five new, rewarding ways you can love your body.

1.

2.

3.

4.

5.

Embrace Compassionate Self-Care

Compassionate self-care means being as kind to yourself as you wouldto someone you dearly love. Instead of judging your behavior or condemning yourself for your behavior, try understanding what caused it and forgiving yourself for a simple misstep. Resolve to work on other ways to better manage your emotions (as you're learning here), and then release all guilt.

Write about the underlying emotion that led you to self-harm.

How could you address that emotion differently next time?

Write a compassionate note to yourself, stating that you understand and forgive yourself for this misstep.

"You've been criticizing yourself for years and it hasn't worked. Try approving of yourself and see what happens."

– LOUISE HAY, SPEAKER AND AUTHOR

List five major reasons your body deserves appreciation.

1.

2.

3.

4.

5.

List five ways to pamper (thank) your body, then follow through with your list.

1.

2.

3.

4.

5.

Note: If overeating or overdrinking remains an ongoing issue, please consult with your doctor and consider outside help.

Forget Dieting, Think Healthy

Dieting holds so many negative connotations (including deprivation and punishment) and rarely achieves long-term success—typically you succeed while on the diet, but then go back to your old eating habits and regain some or all the weight when you stop it. The best way to consistently nurture your body is to change your attitude from indulgence to making healthy choices.

How many times have you dieted in the past? Which diets?

How did you feel if you gained the weight back?

What have you learned from these experiences?

Write about your relationship with food. Do you see a pattern?

Do you have a secret food stash?

What's your guilty pleasure?

Are you ready to commit to choosing what you eat or drink based on the priority of nurturing your body?

"To recognize one's own insanity is, of course, the arising of sanity, the beginning of healing and transcendence."

– ECKHART TOLLE, SPIRITUAL TEACHER AND AUTHOR

List five eating or drinking habits that self-sabotage your efforts to be healthy.

1.
2.
3.
4.
5.

Now it's time to think about how you can avoid those center grocery aisles and make healthier choices.

List five vegetables you like and could add to your meals.

1.
2.
3.
4.
5.

List five fruits you like and could eat more often.

1.
2.
3.
4.
5.

List five unhealthy foods you could limit.

1.
2.
3.
4.
5.

List five unhealthy drinks you could limit.

1.
2.
3.
4.
5.

You can still have your guilty pleasure occasionally, since the point is to commit to your health, not your waistline. Why do you *want* to be healthier? Write about your reasons.

Write a statement *committing* to a healthier way of eating. This commitment is solely for you. You are gifting yourself integration of your intentions with your actions.

List five things you can do to support yourself in that quest. Some examples could be avoiding the center aisles, reading up on nutrition, or learning more about bad fats and processed foods. Create an action plan for facilitating your desire to be healthier and change the *way* you eat, not necessarily *how much* you eat.

1.

2.

3.

4.

5.

Stop Punishing and Start Rewarding

Remember, the more you reward yourself for having the desired thoughts and actions, the more you wire your brain for positivity.

Celebrate every healthier choice you make. Give yourself a star. List five recent choices and pause to pat yourself on the back, buy yourself a rose, reward yourself with a bubble bath. The point is to recognize your healthy choices and reward yourself for them.

1.

2.

3.

4.

5.

"You yourself, as much as anybody in the entire universe, deserve your love and affection."

– BUDDHA

TAKE A SELF-COMPASSION BREAK

Sit comfortably, put your hands over your heart and take a moment to offer your heart protection. Feel the love and warmth of your hands. Say things like, "May I be kind to myself, may I accept myself as I am, may I be understanding and patient with myself," or whatever feels soothing.

Buy yourself the best. If you don't value yourself, no one will. It's one thing to be frugal, but being cheap reinforces feelings of unworthiness. It's better to save up and splurge on the best—because you deserve it.

List five *healthy* foods or drinks that would feel like a treat. Buy yourself the tastiest ones because you deserve them.

1.
2.
3.
4.
5.

List five things you'd love to have and promise yourself that you'll buy the best versions you can afford.

1.
2.
3.
4.
5.

Conquer Your Emotions

The more you learn to modulate your emotions, the easier it will be to choose and develop healthy eating and exercising habits. Begin by identifying the emotional triggers that sabotage your attempts.

List five things friends or family do, or say, that trigger negative emotions.

1.

2.

3.

4.

5.

"Never pull away suddenly from a negative thought or experience. Stay with it until you are indifferent to it or until it turns beautiful. Look at it, love it, then let it go."

– THADDEUS GOLAS,

THE LAZY MAN'S GUIDE TO ENLIGHTENMENT

List five ways you can view their actions differently and thus better handle your challenging emotions the next time.

1.

2.

3.

4.

5.

List any emotions that often result in abusing your body.

1.

2.

3.

4.

5.

Do you see a pattern? Write about it.

List five negative emotions you feel too often.

1.

2.

3.

4.

5.

Spend three minutes thinking about the genesis of those feelings. Do you see a pattern emerging? Write about it.

List five ways to lessen the impact.

1.

2.

3.

4.

5.

List five things you could do to not abuse your body when you feel sad, mad, angry, or other negative emotions.

1.

2.

3.

4.

5.

Make a list of five compassionate statements that will soothe you in future situations.

1.

2.

3.

4.

5.

[3-MINUTE ACTIVITY]

PRACTICE A BREATHING TECHNIQUE TO HELP CALM YOUR EMOTIONS.

SLOW breathing technique. To slow your breathing, sit comfortably. Slowly breathe in from the base of your belly, slowly drawing in breath to the count of ten. Hold the breath to the count of ten, then slowly release your breath to the count of ten. Repeat this until you feel calm.

Choose Activities That Don't Involve Food

We all make eating or drinking the primary way we gather with friends. How about doing something that doesn't involve that instead?

List five things you can do that don't involve food, particularly when you feel the need to self-soothe.

1.

2.

3.

4.

5.

tip

GO ON A HIKE

In a Stanford study, neuroscientists discovered that spending 1½ hours on a hike in a wooded area reduced negative rumination.

List five things you could do with friends that don't involve eating in a restaurant.

1.

2.

3.

4.

5.

Do Activities You Love

As children, most of us spent hours playing, but as adults, we forget to include activities that we love. Not only is it good to enjoy doing something, but it also often involves moving your body, which sure beats watching tv on your couch.

List five activities you loved growing up.

1.
2.
3.
4.
5.

List five ways you can do something similar again.

1.
2.
3.
4.
5.

Make a commitment to choose activity over sedentary activities.

SIX WAYS EXERCISE BENEFITS YOUR POSITIVITY

You don't have to work out at a gym to benefit from movement. Doing something you love that also involves physical movement has immediate positivity benefits, including:

- Reducing muscle tension, so you feel more relaxed.
- Producing more endorphins, which bolsters your sense of well-being.
- Producing more serotonin that helps you feel positive and optimistic.
- Improving concentration and memory.
- Bolstering self-esteem.
- Helping you better manage anxiety.

Wire your brain for pleasure: Forget burning calories, focus on having fun!

Move Your Fantastic Body Every Day

We only need to take seven thousand steps per day to be healthy. On the days you can't even work those in, you still move throughout the day. Yes, picking your clothes off your floor to hang them up, vacuuming, and even walking up a flight of stairs counts. Take an assessment of how much you're moving your body.

List five ways you moved your body today.

1.

2.

3.

4.

5.

Evaluate how much you're falling short. Is that okay with you? Why or why not?

List five new ways you can easily move your body each day.

1.

2.

3.

4.

5.

"Play refreshes and fuels a long-term adult relationship... it is like oxygen: pervasive and mostly unnoticed, but essential to intimacy."

– STUART BROWN, M.D., *PLAY*

List 3 things you are willing to do to improve your health by moving more. Commit to doing them.

1.

tip

DANCE PARTY

Turn on a badass song, leap up, and dance—it releases happiness hormones.

2.

3.

Make a list of five activities that involve movement that you've never done but would like to try. Do them!

1.

2.

3.

4.

5.

FIND YOUR MOTIVATION

According to *Runner's World*, there are four types of runners: the exerciser, the competitor, the enthusiast, and the socializer. The exerciser focuses on the health benefits, the competitor focuses on being the best, the enthusiast enjoys the act of running, and the socializer wants to hang out with other runners. What motivates you? Take three minutes to contemplate and then use what you discover to motivate you to be active more often.

Body-Image Positivity

The days where body shaming seemed socially acceptable are diminishing. More women, and men, are living loud and proud in their bodies. Soft and curvy is definitely in. If you're still hiding your body, feeling like you *should* lose ten or twenty or forty pounds before you really start to live, it's time to get on the body-loving, no-waiting (weighting) bullet train to happiness.

How was your body image formed?

When were you first aware of your body's magnificence?

When did you first feel embarrassed about your body?

List five ways you criticize your body.

1.
2.
3.
4.
5.

List five things your magnificent body does for you.

1.

2.

3.

4.

5.

Find a picture of yourself as a child, write to her, tell her what you love about her, and make sure to end by telling her that you love her *just the way she is*.

"I definitely have body issues, but everybody does. When you come to the realization that everybody does that—even the people that I consider flawless—then you can start to live with the way you are."

– TAYLOR SWIFT, SINGER/SONGWRITER

Tell Advertisers to "Kiss Off"

Keep in mind that corporations invest billions of dollars in developing beauty and health products, then spend millions of dollars to hire Madison Avenue advertising executives who create ads designed to sell those products. Their ads are often designed to make us feel "less than" or that we need to look better to be happy or successful in life, work, and love. They're selling a product. It's up to you to ignore them.

Name five beauty ads that offend you and say why.

1.

2.

3.

4.

5.

Refute or rewrite their message to make it positive.

1.

2.

3.

4.

5.

Love yourself, just the way you are. Practice looking in the mirror and noticing your best assets. State them aloud, "I have unique, magnetic blue eyes; my brown eyes are deep and soulful; my lips are full and luscious; my strong chin reflects my character; my hair is thick and lustrous." Enjoy your unique beauty. Repeat this exercise regularly until you believe yourself (and not the advertisers).

> "Advertising is the art of convincing people to spend money they don't have for things they don't need."
>
> – WILL ROGERS, AMERICAN HUMORIST

"Our earliest messages were how we judged ourselves, how we knew if we were okay or loved or worthwhile. They came from outside in, and the more they were repeated, the more strongly we owned them. They became imprinted on our subconscious to be heard over and over again."

– RUTH FISHEL,
LEARNING TO LIVE IN THE NOW

4

Self Positivity

Your self is not the ego you present to the world; it's the self you may have learned to hide at an early age—your true essence, the self you would be if you could be your best, most open, loving, and secure self. We form our ego in childhood, in accordance with who we think we must be to flourish (or sometimes simply survive) in our family. As we leave home and grow into maturity, we encounter people and situations that help us grow. We also change our self-image as we gather confidence about our own positive qualities and abilities.

The more we succeed in our new world, the more we gain confidence and the kind of self-esteem that bolsters growth. Eventually, we will surrender those parts of our limited ego that no longer serve us and operate from our unlimited, true self.

Developing self positivity will bolster your efforts to start living life as who you truly are, rather than who you learned to be. Let's discuss the various aspects of becoming your authentic self and how you can use positivity to master them.

How Was Your Sense of Self Formed?

- Describe how your parents played a significant role in your developing self.

- Who else played a role in how you came to see your self?

- Write about the positive and negative attributes they assigned to you.

- How did you integrate them into how you thought about your self as a child?

Who Do You Want to Be?

Even if you're not caught up in the wrong profession, take time to consider who your authentic self wants to be.

What would your ideal self be like?

What would you do for work?

Where would you live? How would you live?

What values would mean the most to you?

What choices are you willing to make to honor those values?

"The more you sense the rareness and value of your own life, the more you realize that how you use it, how you manifest it, is all your responsibility. We face such a big task, so naturally we sit down for a while [and meditate on who and where we are]."

– KOBUN CHINO OTOGAWA, ZEN PRIEST

List five things you can do now to start honoring your deepest values.

1.

2.

3.

4.

5.

FEELING "OFF" OR NOT YOURSELF

We've all used that excuse when we don't like how we're behaving, but you are always you. In truth, when you feel "off," you're simply not thinking, feeling, or acting in alignment with how you think of yourself or want others to think of your ideal self. Your autobiographical self (personality, identity, true self) is not set in stone. Each day your cerebral cortex and your brain stem stitch together the self you'll be taking into the world each day—and you can choose what it will be.

[3-MINUTE ACTIVITY]

TRY A ZAZEN MEDITATION

Zazen means "seated meditation" in Japanese. To practice Zazen meditation, take three minutes to sit comfortably. Keep your back straight from pelvis to neck, and cast your eyes softly downward. Breathe slowly in and out and allow all thoughts to pass through your mind. Notice your thoughts but do not attach or dwell on them. Try thinking about "not thinking," a state the Japanese believe allows thoughts to pass without attaching to them, allowing you to simply "be" in the present.

Don't Believe Something That Isn't True

Is it true, or only what your anxious mind thinks? We all have that nagging inner voice who critiques and criticizes our decisions and actions. Unfortunately, we often simply believe this inner voice and accept its judgments as truth, which can lead to negative self-assessments, and even depression. It helps to realize that the words or images going through your anxious mind are just that: thoughts and images. They may or may not be true.

List five misconceptions your anxious mind has believed about yourself.

1.

2.

3.

4.

5.

"Your consciousness is actually experiencing your mental model of reality, not reality itself."

– MICHAEL A. SINGER, *THE UNTETHERED SOUL*

Write the counterargument for each.

1.

2.

3.

tip

HELPFUL THOUGHTS

Whether your thoughts and judgments about yourself are true or not, what matters most is whether they are helpful. If they're not helpful, stop listening to them and focus more on those that benefit you and your quest for growth.

4.

5.

[3-MINUTE ACTIVITY]

TRY THE LEAF MEDITATION

Sit comfortably and breathe slowly in and out. When ready, mindfully focus your attention on negative thoughts you have about yourself. Imagine placing them, one by one, onto a leaf. Imagine placing the leaf on a flowing stream of water and allowing it to drift away.

Think about an anxious thought or personal judgment you often make about yourself, one your nagging inner critic voices often. Try a 3-minute, clarifying meditation, in which you examine that thought. What was my anxious mind telling me about myself? What thoughts are going through my mind right now? Are these thoughts true or distorted? What is the truth?

Take three minutes to write about what you discovered in the meditation.

Were your thoughts accurate? Why not?

Were your thoughts helpful in any way?

What judgments were you hearing?

Were the judgments fair? Helpful?

Is there a negative benefit you get from believing these negative thoughts and judgements?

Formulate more accurate statements about yourself.

Understand How Cognitive Dissonance Works

Cognitive dissonance is holding two beliefs at the same time, when both cannot be true—justifying smoking when you know it's bad for you, stealing small items from work to compensate for being unappreciated, or lying to someone you love to "protect" them. This dissonance causes discomfort, a nagging feeling that you're not being true to yourself, not honoring or abiding by the knowledge, beliefs, and values that you consider imperative. Typically, you find ways to justify the unacceptable behavior. An example might be staying in an abusive relationship and justifying it with irrational excuses.

"Myths, whether in written or visual form, serve a vital role of asking unanswerable questions and providing unquestionable answers. Most of us, most of the time, have a low tolerance for ambiguity and uncertainty. We want to reduce the cognitive dissonance of not knowing by filling the gaps with answers."

– MICHAEL SHERMER, *THE MORAL ARC*

Is there an area in your life where you are experiencing cognitive dissonance?

List the top three excuses you make to continue these behaviors.

1.

2.

3.

Do they seem rational? Can you identify the ones that aren't rational?

Which ones are you willing to change, for the sake of feeling better about yourself and reducing cognitive dissonance?

SEEING CLEARLY MATTERS

Someone in an abusive relationship often uses cognitive dissonance as their primary defense mechanism. They often justify staying in the relationship by convincing herself that she's not seeing clearly or that "they love me as best they can," or that "it's only because they're under so much stress" (it will get better when...). Until the person being abused resolves to clearly see her justifications as delusion, cognitive dissonance may be the least of her worries.

How Do You Make You Feel Good About Your Self?

You reinforce your new authentic self by doing and saying what you honestly believe, according to your values, regardless of undesired outcomes, and then recognizing that you feel best when doing so.

List five things you do that supports who you want to be.

1. ______

2. ______

3. ______

4. ______

5. ______

"What you notice, give your attention to, talk about, get all worked up over emotionally is what you are inviting into your life, whether you mean to or not."

– CATHERINE PONDER,
OPEN YOUR MIND TO RECEIVE

List five things you could do to further support your authentic self.

1.

2.

3.

4.

5.

List five ways you'll reward your authentic self for living according to your values.

1.

2.

3.

4.

5.

Write Your New Concept of Self

Martin Seligman, PhD, founder of Positive Psychology, and author of *Authentic Happiness* studied more than two hundred books written over the last three thousand years and concluded that genuine happiness comes from using our inherent, signature strengths (inborn talents or psychological characteristics) to execute positive, meaningful action. When you aren't operating from your strengths for positivity, he believes you feel inauthentic.

Clean the negative slate. Write down at least five negative thoughts you've held in past, then breathe and release them.

1. ______________________________

2. ______________________________

3. ______________________________

4. ______________________________

5. ______________________________

> "One's own self is well hidden from one's own self; of all mines of treasure, one's own is the last to be dug up."
>
> – NIETZSCHE, PHILOSOPHER

List at least five new positives to replace them. Be specific and choose qualities that make you proud of who you are.

1.

2.

3.

4.

5.

We live in a superficial culture, in which people are judged on surface qualities rather than depth. List five ways you've judged yourself based on superficial qualities or ideals.

1.

2.

3.

4.

5.

Self-Love Positivity

If you love your self, it helps others to also love you. Everyone will see how you treat yourself with love and respect, honoring your boundaries, caring for your psyche and your body, choosing to do what's most important to you, and fostering loving relationships. These admirable qualities will boost your self-esteem, and we all know how it's connected to not only what we accomplish in life, but how happy we feel.

To love yourself, you'll need to surrender all shame and guilt. Self-love means choosing to make yourself feel good and making yourself a priority bolsters self-esteem. Disrupt your tendencies to punish yourself for perceived failings. Discover the huge benefit that comes from focusing on the positive. Then forgive yourself for everything you ever said that denigrated your sense of self.

Growing up, what made you feel good about yourself?

What made you feel "less than" others?

"This life is mine alone. So, I have stopped asking people for directions to places they've never been."

– GLENNON DOYLE, AUTHOR

Is it okay to be ordinary? Why or why not?

List five ways to boost your opinion of yourself.

1.

2.

3.

4.

5.

List ten things you like about your self. Write them as affirmations to reinforce positivity.

1.

2.

3.

4.

5.

6.

7.

8.

9.

10.

Always accentuate the positive. Ban negative self-talk. Reframe all negative comments to positive ones. Write five negative things you say about yourself and reframe them to be positive. Example: “I always fail at everything I try.” Changed to: “I am someone who loves to try new things and I am willing to fail because I always try again.”

1.

2.

3.

4.

5.

Celebrate your self. Wire your brain to connect growth with pleasure. Write about ways you can celebrate yourself.

Practice Positive Self-talk

Every time you criticize yourself, turn it around and say something positive instead—reframing how you view yourself.

List ten statements you can make about yourself that are both true and complimentary.

1.

2.

3.

4.

5.

6.

7.

8.

9.

10.

Transform those statements into affirmations and say them regularly.

PRACTICE RADICAL SELF-COMPASSION

Rather than feeling sorry for someone, Buddhists feel profound empathy. They focus on the other person's situation, understand their motivations, acknowledge their mistakes, and forgive them. This comes from knowing that the person has done the best they can, at that moment in time, with the knowledge they had. Take three minutes to remember something you did that made you feel bad about yourself, offer yourself radical self-compassion, and do better next time.

Love Yourself the Way You Love Others

Take the Unmitigated Communion Scale test by Fritz and Helgeson to figure out if you spend too much time caring about others and not enough time caring about yourself. Answer the following questions about how you relate to friends and family. Be truthful, on a scale of one to five, with 1 being (strongly disagree); 2 (slightly disagree); 3 (neither agree nor disagree); 4 (slightly agree); 5 (strongly agree).

____ I place the needs of others above my own.

____ I find myself getting overly involved in others' problems.

____ For me to be happy, I need others to be happy.

____ I worry about how other people get along without me when I am not there.

____ I have great difficulty getting to sleep at night when other people are upset.

____ It's impossible for me to satisfy my own needs when they interfere with the needs of others.

____ I can't say no when someone asks me for help.

____ Even when exhausted, I will always help other people.

____ I often worry about others' problems.

After you've recorded your responses, add up the numbers and divide by nine to get your mean score. Scores above 3 indicate that your caring is lopsided. You need to think more about yourself, and a little less about others.

"Love yourself first, and everything else falls into line. You really have to love yourself to get anything done in this world."

– LUCILLE BALL, ACTRESS AND PRODUCER

Love Yourself Unconditionally

Unconditional love means that you don't impose standards on yourself. Reasonable expectations are fine, but not qualifiers.

List five things you punish yourself for doing. Promise to love yourself despite these behaviors.

1.

2.

3.

4.

5.

Think about people you love. List five specific ways you show your love to them, now show that same love to yourself.

1.

2.

3.

4.

5.

It's okay to tell yourself you're fabulous, every day! Write five affirmations and say them daily to boost your self-esteem.

1.

2.

3.

4.

5.

"To love oneself is the beginning of a lifelong romance."

– OSCAR WILDE, PLAYWRIGHT

Pamper Yourself

Yes, you deserve pampering. In fact, pampering is the ideal way to reward yourself for all the changes you're working to make.

Make a list of ways you can pamper yourself. Be imaginative and specific. Pick a beauty day and spend it totally pampering your body. Make an appointment for a massage, a mani-pedi, a mud bath, a spa treatment, a haircut, or whatever suits your fancy.

1.

2.

3.

4.

5.

"When dealing with people, remember you are not dealing with creatures of logic, but creatures of emotion."

– DALE CARNEGIE, AUTHOR

5

Relationship Positivity

It's a simple fact that no one enjoys being around someone who's always negative, depressed, critical, judgmental, or angry. If you're someone who thinks positively, practices positivity, and focuses on the good in life, others will naturally be drawn to you. It's also important that you develop social skills that foster intimacy. One crucial aspect of that is developing your ability to feel compassion for others.

Be Compassionate toward Others

Try Cognitive Reframing: Think about a time when someone behaved badly. Imagine what might have happened in their life that would have caused them to behave so badly. Think about what they might need to foster healing. Write it down but DO NOT offer it to them. Instead, send the person loving vibes, and the next time you see their destructive pattern and its aftermath, offer him compassionate constraint. Sometimes it's helpful to say, "I can see you are having a difficult time." Or "I'm sorry this is so hard for you." Or "You seem incredibly frustrated, can I help?"

Always pause to consider the other person's point of view. Think about the last disagreement you had at work. Write about it from the other person's point of view, imagining what motivated him or her to see it differently. This bolsters healthy empathy—being able to identify with others' pain.

If you find yourself constantly feeling frustrated at work, pause every time it happens and jot down notes about your feelings. This helps you notice how often you're falling into the negative trap. And what needs to improve.

Write about negative thoughts you had at work recently.

Write how you could turn those negative thoughts into positive ones.

List any actions you need to take to effect change.

Become a Better Listener

Listening closely when someone else speaks is an art few practice these days. If you want to be a better friend or coworker, learning to listen closely is paramount. Basically, five steps for improving attentive listening are:

1. Find the proper environment. If someone has something important to tell you, seek a quiet place, with no interruptions, and turn off your phone.
2. Look into the eyes of the other person, but also be sensitive to their body language and adjust if they seem uncomfortable with the intensity of your look, or the amount of space between you.
3. Be fully present, stop all interfering thoughts, and truly pay attention to what the person is saying. Most of us only half listen.
4. Wait for natural breaks to ask questions. Occasionally validate what you are hearing them say. "So, you are telling me that you feel..."
5. Avoid offering solutions. Most often, people just want someone to truly listen and care. When they are done speaking, you can gently ask if they'd like to know what you think or what you'd do in a similar situation.

Truly listening is the best way to show someone how much you value them. Giving someone your full attention deepens connections.

Have you ever been guilty of not listening when a friend or family member talks about something important? What happened? How did it make you feel?

How does it feel when someone you value doesn't listen carefully to what you're saying? Write about one incident.

List three things you could say to encourage someone to listen more closely.

1.

2.

3.

HUG OFTEN AND LONGER

Four hugs a day has been proven to boost emotional and physical health (eight are even better), but hugs need to last at least six seconds. That's how long it takes for your brain to release oxytocin, the happiness hormone. The longer you hug, the happier you'll feel.

Build a Network of Positive-Minded Friends

Share positive energy. Just as "Debbie Downer" can bring everyone down, being surrounded by positivity reinforces positivity. Choose friends who focus on the positive, trend heavily towards an optimistic viewpoint, and believe in themselves.

List five people you know right now who fit this model.

1.

2.

3.

4.

5.

“My best friend is the one who brings out the best in me.”

– HENRY FORD, *INVENTOR*

List five ideas for spending more time with them. For example, plan a fun event during which you’ll thank them for being so...positive!

1.

2.

3.

4.

5.

Jettison Negative Friends

If their negativity is always bringing you down, or if most of their criticism is directed at you, you may want to jettison these people from your intimate circle.

List any friends who tend to criticize and write about the ways they disrespect you.

"No person is your friend who demands your silence or denies your right to grow."

– ALICE WALKER, AUTHOR

Assess how you think each would respond to you setting boundaries.

Try setting boundaries, but if they cannot reform, consider jettisoning them. Bad energy brings you down. List any ideas on how you can set boundaries with each person.

Appreciate Your Supportive Friends

As you've learned, positive reinforcement builds positivity. Most of us appreciate our friends, but we may not tell them just how much often enough. Everyone loves to be appreciated.

List the ways supportive friends help you love yourself. Pause to appreciate their support when it happens. State your appreciation aloud.

"Let us be grateful to people who make us happy; they are the charming gardeners who make our souls blossom."

– MARCEL PROUST, AUTHOR

Handwrite a note to a friend to express your gratitude. Few people handwrite notes, so receiving one makes a big impression. If it's a friend, choosing a lovely card boosts impact. If it's a coworker, you can use sticky notes or index cards. The point is to reinforce their good behavior and make yourself feel better. It doesn't have to be a big thing, maybe they brought you a coffee. Find something that you appreciated and thank them for their thoughtfulness. Bonus: two people feel good.

Find more friends like them. List five places you can make new friends.

1.

2.

3.

4.

5.

Focus on What Matters

Instead of complimenting friends and family on their appearance, how about focusing on their positive traits—those things they do that make you feel good, their professional accomplishments, how they're improving themselves, their interests and community spirit, how they bring sunshine into other people's lives.

List five people you see regularly.

1.

2.

3.

4.

5.

"Spend time thinking of what you want rather than what you don't want."

– SANAYA ROMAN,
PERSONAL POWER THROUGH AWARENESS

List ways you could compliment them that has nothing to do with their appearance. Examples could be, "She is always dependable and trustworthy." Or "She's very empathetic towards anyone who feels hurt."

1.

2.

3.

4.

5.

Now turn those same positive statements around and write them about yourself. "I am always dependable and trustworthy." "I am very empathetic towards anyone who feels bad." Write them down. It matters!

1.

2.

3.

4.

5.

Practice Social Media Positivity

Instead of presenting a false self on social media, or comparing yourself to others doing so, either cut back altogether or post things that are positive, uplifting, and true. You don't need to be "special." Being ordinary, yet truly your unique, authentic self is more than enough.

Avoid comparing yourself to impossible standards. Setting expectations too high becomes self-defeating. List at least five ways you've been comparing yourself to others on social media.

1.

2.

3.

4.

5.

Focus on being real and sharing what matters. Being genuine reinforces self. List a few ways you could share more about who you are.

1.

2.

3.

"Comparison is an act of violence against the self."

– IYANLA VANZANT, INSPIRATIONAL AUTHOR

Here are some ways to practice social media positivity:

- Just be you, just the way you are. This reinforces that you are "enough."
- Spend more time thinking about yourself. We spend too much time worrying about what others think about us, when, in fact, most people are far too self-absorbed to be thinking about you anyway.
- Be kind to yourself and others. Kindness generates happiness.
- Block the "Debbie Downers" in your life and engage more often with those who radiate positivity.

WHY LOVE IS BLIND

When your existing beliefs and your level of desire contradict what available evidence supports, you may deceive yourself into believing what you want to see. Because subjective emotions create strong feelings, they may hamper your ability to process objective evidence. Love tends to redirect and refocus our attention solely on the positive attributes of the person we desire.

[3-MINUTE ACTIVITY]

TRY A HEART MEDITATION

Sit in a comfortable position, focus on your breath, release all thoughts, place your hand over your heart, and focus your attention on your heart. For three minutes, simply listen to your heart and see if it has any messages for you. Then think or speak affirmations, such as: "My heart is open to love. I love myself and others. I love and forgive those who have hurt me. I ask for loving forgiveness. I send love into the world. I invite love into my life," or whatever feels right to you. Ease back into your fully awake and alert mode and keep that heart open!

"When we truly
choose to care
about something,
change
always happens."

– MEGAN RAPINOE,
USA WOMEN'S
SOCCER TEAM CAPTAIN

6

Self Positivity

If you're going to achieve anything in life, positivity will be essential. You need it to dream forward, formulate plans, anticipate success, and overcome obstacles. Positivity serves as the engine behind the motivation you'll need to pursue what you want.

The mental benefits of positivity often include:

- More creativity
- Greater problem-solving skills
- Clearer thinking
- Better mood
- Better coping skills
- Less depression

List qualities or career goals you'd like to develop:

In the Buddhist tradition, wise intention is a crucial step on the seeker's path to end suffering. They believe emotions and motivations lead to intention, and intention precedes all action. Indeed, all changes are first created in your mind and then created in your environment. Every thought becomes an intention. Thus, it's important to think about and decide what's most important to your sense of self. Work through these tasks, and you'll have a much clearer vision.

Identify five role models for what you want your ideal self to be like.

1.

2.

3.

4.

5.

Identify and list the major steps needed to reach your goals.

1.

2.

3.

4.

5.

6.

7.

8.

Spend three minutes prioritizing the goals, which will you do first?

Break down each major step into "doable chunks." This creates the opportunity for you to succeed all along the way. Remember to celebrate each goal you meet, at least in some small way. This reinforces positivity and goal setting.

"What is given to the eyes is the intention of the soul."

– ARISTOTLE, PHILOSOPHER

Select the first goal you want to achieve and write a plan for mastering the steps required. Everything is easier when it's broken down into steps. Do the easiest part of the task first. Success breeds success.

Review your plan and write down the next five things you'll do in the coming week to bring you closer to achieving your goals.

1.

2.

3.

4.

5.

Remember getting stickers from your teacher? They use them because they work. Go back and draw smiley faces or bright red check marks or whatever makes you happy beside each goal you met. Take a moment to absorb the feeling of success.

Look up a quote that bolsters your new vision of yourself and how you want to think. Write it out and tape it to your mirror. Consider it your daily dose of inspiration.

List five lively, upbeat theme songs—ones that spur you to dance. Play one, jump up and dance, and do this every time you need a boost.

1.

2.

3.

4.

5.

Make a List of Self-Judgments That Hold You Back

As discussed earlier, your own negative self-assessments (that may be based on early life experiences or false perceptions) can sabotage your best efforts.

Make friends with your inner critic. Rather than seeing them as a critic, try seeing them as a part of you who's only trying to help. List the five worst things they whisper under their breath about you.

1.

2.

3.

4.

5.

Take each statement and flip those negatives to positives.

1.

2.

3.

4.

5.

Briefly sympathize with how they think they're helping. Forgive them, thank them, then educate them by creating a list of the true qualities that refute their opinions.

> "You are not a drop in the ocean. You are the entire ocean in a drop."
>
> – RUMI, POET

Practice compassionate self-care instead

List five ways you can more gently encourage yourself to make better choices.

1.

2.

3.

4.

5.

tip

REINFORCE YOUR POSITIVITY

Put a "positivity reminder" in your phone alerts. When it dings, pause for three minutes while you focus on identifying three positive things you can say about yourself. Cross your hands over your heart and say them. Breathe them in and congratulate yourself for reinforcing your positivity.

Write down your intentions for this week.

KEEP YOUR EYE ON THE PRIZE

When you stop focusing on what you want to create, your mind falls sway to rumination, mindless worrying, fantasizing, or zoning out, all of which sabotage your true intention. It's important to write down weekly goals and intentions.

Manage Your Expectations

To boost your chances of success, it's always helpful to make your aspirations (and expectations) achievable, i.e., realistic. Dreaming lofty dreams is great fun—and important—but the path to real growth involves mastering a series of achievable steps.

List five expectations.

1.

2.

3.

4.

5.

Take each expectation down a notch (if needed) to reflect more realistic goals. For example: "I will be manager of my department in three months." Changed to: "I will continue to do my best work, improve my skills, do whatever I can at work to make a positive impression, and ask my boss what is needed to become a manager."

1.

2.

3.

4.

5.

Reframe Failure

Don't be afraid to fail. Failures are an essential step to success. Reframe failure as a learning experience, and you've shifted from negativity to positivity, which will give your next effort a huge advantage.

Write down the last five things you failed.

1.

2.

3.

4.

5.

"Try again. Fail again.
Fail better."

– SAMUEL BECKETT, *PLAYWRIGHT*

What did you learn from each failure?

1.

2.

3.

4.

5.

Write about how you can do better next time.

Stop Idealizing and Idolizing the Wrong People

We tend to idolize beauty over brains, celebrity over accomplishment or financial wealth over altruistic or scientific contributions. We are often focused on the wrong things, and social media has only made it worse.

List five people you idolize for the right reasons.

1.

2.

3.

4.

5.

Write about what makes them admirable.

List five traits these people have that you'd like to develop.

1.

2.

3.

4.

5.

Define Your Idea of a Consequential Person

This would be someone who doesn't fritter away time and focuses on what's important. Even their thoughts are deeper than most.

Why is this person more interesting?

List five ways you can foster more depth. Start doing them.

1.

2.

3.

4.

5.

Identify Your Superpower

What you believe about yourself becomes true, and we all have special talents. You don't have to be a superhero to have a superpower. Maybe your superpower is bringing people together, maybe it's cooking with love, maybe it's capturing people's souls in photographs, or having an acute sense of empathy.

List five things you do well. Elaborate. What makes you so good?

1.

2.

3.

4.

5.

Choose one to be your designated superpower. You don't ever have to tell anyone what it is, but recognizing and acknowledging it will bolster your sense of self. Write about your superpower and how it manifests.

Use Your Imagination to Dream Forward

Imagining and writing about your best probable future creates and bolsters positive emotions.

Set aside three minutes to write about what your ideal, potential future will look like. Stay focused on the positive and only imagine ways that everything could (and will) go right. This will increase optimistic feelings and bolster choices you will make to help it come true.

Take three minutes to meditate and see yourself achieving your goals, living the life you want. Envision how it will look and feel.

Happiness Positivity

To have a wonderful life, you don't need to do anything exceptional. You can simply relish "being happy." If you focus on training your brain and mind to think positively and learn many of the techniques provided, you'll soon be able to sit back and enjoy a happy life.

Revisit Happy Experiences

A 2002 study found that imagining laughter triggered the brain in the same way it would if one just experienced an event that elicited laughter. Thus, merely imagining or remembering a happy time in your life recreates that feeling and, if done repeatedly, can wire your brain for happiness. It's important, however, to truly engage your imagination (or memory) and help your body feel how it felt to laugh or experience immense pleasure.

- Take three minutes to remember a time you felt positively joyful. Take your mind back to the event and draw upon your senses to make it feel like you're there, re-experiencing everything. Try to see what was beautiful, smell what made it luscious, observe what brought you joy. Stay with the memory until you feel it all again.
- Repeat the exercise and make this memory about love.
- Repeat this exercise and make it about someone you love.
- Repeat this exercise and make it about your happiest birthday celebration.

Feel Gratitude for Your Blessings

According to gratitude expert Robert Emmons, gratitude arises from two processes: You recognize that something good happened in your life, and you are fully aware that this "good" was a gift, whether it came from someone else, from the universe, from good fortune, or your own positivity. Focusing on what we are grateful for can be an intentional, even daily habit worth nurturing, and the more you practice writing down your daily list of "things you are grateful for," the more you rewire your brain to focus on the positive.

List five things that happened today that you are grateful for. Pause to acknowledge and feel the blessings.

1.

2.

3.

4.

5.

tip

GRATITUDE JAR

If you don't want to write in a gratitude journal each night, you can try a "gratitude jar." Simply write down one thing you're grateful for each day and drop the slip of paper into the designated jar. At the end of the year, you can pull out the slips, then revisit and celebrate the many good things that happened in your life.

Keep a daily gratitude journal for a week. Write what happened and how good it made you feel. Even if it seems very minor, please include things or moments for which you're grateful.

Create a list of five people who have positively impacted your life and who inspire a sense of thankfulness. Write about them.

1.
2.
3.
4.
5.

Take three minutes to silently focus on sending expressions of gratitude and tidings of goodwill to everyone on the list.

Write a note to anyone on your list and give it to them.

Write a list of five particularly memorable, "good times" in your past. Specify why they were so memorable.

1.
2.
3.
4.
5.

Take a few minutes to remember each, visualizing the scene and calling forth how you felt. This not only reinforces positive feelings, as your body also "re-experiences" those same emotions.

List all the things in your current life for which are grateful. This could be as big as your parents being healthy and your brain being whip-smart to something as small as your dog being well-mannered and the tree in your yard providing fabulous shade.

Meditate for three minutes on all the good in your life. Feel the gratitude and allow it to flood your body with good feelings. Do this often.

EVERYBODY DANCE NOW

Researchers discovered that certain movements, prevalent in many cultures, are inspired by joy: reaching your arms up (like doing the wave in a sport stadium), swaying from side to side, bouncing to a rhythmic beat, or spinning like a dancer with your arms gloriously outstretched. These physical actions don't simply express a feeling of joy; research shows they also elicit joy. If you want to double your pleasure, get a friend to join in. The effects of these joyful movements intensify when you see someone else doing them, proving that happiness is truly contagious.

Welcome Awe into Your Life

According to British biologist and author Richard Dawkins, the feeling of awed wonder that science (and nature) can give us is one of the highest experiences the human psyche can experience. Being awestruck feels so grand, bathes your body and brain in those feel-good chemicals, and it decreases activity in your brain's Default Mode Network (DMN), which reduces mind wandering, rumination, and negative self-judgments. Studies have shown that feeling awestruck also makes us happier, more content with life, more focused on beauty than money, calmer, and humble.

Make a list of five things that make you feel awestruck.

1. ______________________________

2. ______________________________

3. ______________________________

4. ______________________________

5. ______________________________

"Remember to look up at the stars and not down at your feet. Try to make sense of what you see and wonder about what makes the universe exist. Be curious."

– STEPHEN HAWKING

Write about the last time you experienced awe and include sensual details.

Meditate for three minutes and revisit that experience, focusing on the sensual aspects of how it felt to experience awe. Notice how your body feels when focusing on awe. Remember, deep remembering is like experiencing the moment all over again, which offers all those good feelings to your brain and body again.

Use your imagination to think of five places you could go to experience awe.

1.

2.

3.

4.

5.

Think of people that produce awe and list them. It could be teachers, nurses, explorers, gardeners, musicians, your local food bank, your free library, firefighters, policewomen, or your grandmother.

1.

2.

3.

4.

5.

Take a walk in your neighborhood and look for the awe around you (architecture, plants, animals, the petals of a flower, the persistence of a bee). Snap photos so you can view them later and re-experience the awe all over again.

Focus on Serving Others

The less you focus on yourself, the happier you'll be.

List five ways you can, or do, serve others in your intimate circle.

1.

2.

3.

4.

5.

"Everybody can be great because anybody can serve. You don't have to have a college degree to serve. You don't have to make your subject and verb agree to serve. You only need a heart full of grace. A soul generated by love."

– MARTIN LUTHER KING JR., MINISTER AND ACTIVIST

Search online for five volunteer opportunities in your neighborhood. Consider one.

1.

2.

3.

4.

5.

Search online for five charities in your city. Create a plan for giving.

1.

2.

3.

4.

5.

List five ways you can be a more thoughtful person.

1.

2.

3.

4.

5.

List five ways you can be a more generous person.

1.

2.

3.

4.

5.

Find Your Passion and Pursue It

When we love what we do, we are happy. Finding your passion is about identifying what truly matters to you and then finding ways to incorporate it into your life.

Identify the top five things you feel passionately about. State why you care so deeply.

1.

2.

3.

4.

5.

List five ways you can bring more of what truly matters to you into your life.

1.

2.

3.

4.

5.

Focus on Creating an Adventurous Life

Feelings of excitement boost positive energy and help you expand your world.

What five new things would you like to try? Roller skating? Speed dating? Writing classes? Surfing? Creating a travel blog?

1.

2.

3.

4.

5.

List five things you LOVE to do. Do them.

1.

2.

3.

4.

5.

Plan something you've never done before. When doing it, savor the moment, pay attention to how it feels. Take in the good.

Write about it. Re-experiencing positive experiences reinforces happiness.

GET YOUR GROOVE ON

Researchers have found that listening to music stimulates the same pleasure centers in your brain as enjoying sex or eating a delicious meal do. Any music that gets you going, elicits a strong positive emotion, sends chills up your spine (in a good way), or moves you onto the dance floor will boost your mood. Even if you simply pause to truly listen to the music, it will boost positivity.

Enjoy Your Life as It Is

Joyfulness is a choice.

List five things you've done recently that brought you joy. What made them so much fun?

1.

2.

3.

4.

5.

Write more about the top three things that brought you joy. What was happening? Who was there?

1.

2.

3.

What was it about those experiences that made them so much fun?

Stop Waiting and Just Be Happy

As we've learned, positivity comes when you know more about yourself, know more about your values, know more about the roots of your emotions and how you react to emotions, know how to better manage your emotions, know how to love yourself and others, and know how to grow. Now that you've garnered a lot of wisdom, it's time to put what you've learned into action. As you do, you'll not only radiate positivity, but you'll also feel happier every day.

"Now and then it's good to pause in our pursuit of happiness and just be happy."

– GUILLAUME APOLLINAIRE, POET

RECOMMENDED WEBSITES

The Art of Simple. https://www.theartofsimple.net/.

Daily Good. https://www.dailygood.org/.

National Institute of Mental Health. https://www.nimh.nih.gov/.

Pasricha, Neil. "The Top 1000." 1000 Awesome Things. https://1000awesomethings.com/the-top-1000/.

Pease, Kelly. Happsters. https://happsters.com/.

Rubin, Gretchen. Gretchen Rubin. https://gretchenrubin.com/.

Sobczak, Connie, Elizabeth Scott. The Body Positive. https://thebodypositive.org/.

Story Corps. https://storycorps.org/.

Weis-Corbley, Geri. Good News Network. https://www.goodnewsnetwork.org/.

RESOURCES

Aubele, Teresa, Susan Reynolds, and Stan Wenck. *Train Your Brain to Get Happy: The Simple Program That Primes Your Gray Cells for Joy, Optimism, and Serenity*. Massachusetts: Adams Media, 2011.

Brach, Tara. *Radical Compassion: Learning to Love Yourself and Your World with the Practice of RAIN*. New York: Viking, 2019.

Brown, Brené. *Atlas of the Heart: Mapping Meaningful Connection and the Language of Human Experience*. United States: Random House, 2021.

Burns, David. *Feeling Great: The Revolutionary New Treatment for Depression and Anxiety*. United States: PESI Publishing, 2020.

Clement Stone, W., and Napoleon Hill. *Success Through a Positive Mental Attitude*. New York: Pocket Books, 1960.

D. West, Zachary. *Positive Thinking How to Change Your Negative Mindset on Life, Build the Habit of Positive Thoughts and Live a Happy and Successful Life*. United States: CreateSpace, 2016.

Fosslien, Liz, and Mollie West Duffy. *Big Feelings: How to Be Okay When Things Are Not Okay.* United States: Portfolio, 2022.

Graziano Breuning, Loretta. *The Science of Positivity: Stop Negative Thought Patterns by Changing Your Brain Chemistry*. Massachusetts: Adams Media, 2017.

Hanc, John, Margaret Moore, and Edward Phillips. *Organize Your Emotions, Optimize Your Life: Decode Your Emotional DNA—and Thrive*. United States: William Morrow, 2016.

Hay, Louise. *Mirror Work: 21 Days to Heal Your Life. United States:* Hay House, 2016.

J. Siegel, Daniel, Jack Kornfield. *Mindfulness and the Brain: A Professional Training in the Science and Practice of Meditative Awareness.* Colorado: Sounds True, 2010.

Kabat-Zinn, Jon. *Mindfulness for Beginners: Reclaiming the Present Moment and Your Life.* Colorado: Sounds True, 2012.

Kaplan Thaler, Linda, and Robin Koval. *Grit to Great: How Perseverance, Passion, and Pluck Take You from Ordinary to Extraordinary.* New York: Crown Business, 2015.

Klein, Stefan. *The Science of Happiness: How Our Brains Make Us Happy—and What We Can Do to Get Happier.* New York: Da Capo Lifelong, 2006.

Kornfield, Jack. *Meditation for Beginners.* Mumbai: Jaico Publishing House, 2010.

Neff, Kristin. *Fierce Self-Compassion: How Women Can Harness Kindness to Speak Up, Claim Their Power, and Thrive.* United States: Harper Wave, 2021.

Norman Vincent Peale, Norman. *The Power of Positive Thinking: Ten Traits for Maximum Results.* United States: Touchstone, 2003.

Paquette, Jonah. *Awestruck: How Embracing Wonder Can Make You Happier, Healthier, and More Connected*. Colorado: Shambhala Publications, 2020.